BEHIND THE MASK

Behind the Mask

An Introvert's Perspective on Trauma, Perseverance, and Healing

DR. CHRISTAL L. CHATMAN

SMS Ministries Publishing

Contents

DEDICATION

FOREWARD

PREFACE

1	The Discovery	16
2	My Journey	30
3	Where Was God?	44
4	I'm OK	59
5	The Day	72

6	Time to Heal	84
References		96

ABOUT THE AUTHOR

Copyright © 2022 by Dr. Christal Chatman. All rights reserved. Written permission must be secured from the publisher to use or reproduce any part of this book, except for brief quotations in critical reviews or articles.

Published by SMS Ministries in Killeen, Texas. First Printing, 2022

Edited by Michelle L. Massie Early for ProEditor at www.proeditor.us.

Cover Design by Ben Consulting at bnconsulting.info@gmail.com.

SMS Ministries books may be purchased in bulk for educational, business, fundraising, or sales promotional use.

For information please email publishing@SMSMinistries.co.

Scriptures taken from the Holy Bible, New International Version®, NIV®. Copyright © 1973, 1978, 1984, 2011 by Biblica, Inc.™ Used by permission of Zondervan. All rights reserved worldwide. www.zondervan.com The "NIV" and "New International Version" are trademarks registered in the United States Patent and Trademark Office by Biblica, Inc.™

ISBN: 978-1-7350847-3-2

Dedication

John aka "Snack" – You are the extrovert to my introvert in so many wonderful ways! Thank you for your support and encouragement as I embark on this journey toward fulfilling God's purpose for my life. Loving you and being loved by you brings joy to my heart.

Mom, Dad, and Jimmy – Thank you for being my biggest cheerleaders! Mom and Dad, my prayer is that my life always makes you proud! Jimmy, as I share in all of your amazing accomplishments, you are my inspiration to keep pushing, striving, and growing. OHHHHH, and thank you for the laughs! There is NOTHING like one of our family dinners.

Brent – Kiddo, I love you with my whole heart. I hope that my life shows you that you can accomplish anything that you set your mind to do. It may not always be easy, but with Christ, you will find the strength to do all things. Be teachable. Be strong and courageous. Keep allowing God to use the anointing on your life to change the world!

Sissy – I do not have adequate words to express how I feel about you! I love you more than David's sunflower seeds, French fries, and C&P crab legs! We are quite a pair... not judging, but totally judging... guaranteed laughter until tears... upset, but totally still friends forever... quiet for too long, expect a call or text... Seriously, thank you for bringing this God-assignment to life for me. Love you!!!

To my angels on earth aka My Friends and Sisters – Thank you for allowing God to use you to save my life! My friendship with each of you is incredibly special to me. As you pursue God's purpose for your life, I am always here to pray for you, support you, and cheer for you along the journey. Dream big! Go for it!

Foreword

When asked to be part of this project, I didn't know where to begin. There's so much I can say about *Behind the Mask* and Dr. Christal L. Chatman. It took me longer than usual to gather my thoughts because I wanted my introduction to this text and its author to be perfect. That's when it hit me... nobody is perfect, and nobody has it all together all the time. That's not only where we will begin, but that's what you will see throughout this book.

Life often throws us curveballs and we don't know how to manage them. Some people lash out, some people suppress, and others simply ignore their issues. I believe we can all take a little time to evaluate why we respond the way we do. In this book, you will hear Dr. Chatman's heart as she shares her journey of self-discovery and healing through the lens of her personality type.

"I AM AN INTROVERT," Dr. Chatman resolutely declares at the beginning of nearly every chapter. Can you imagine walking through life not understanding your aversion to large crowds, why you're reluctant to make new friends, or why you feel as if you are socially awkward? Can you imagine going through your adolescent and even adult years trying to figure out why you still have some issues expressing yourself freely and honestly with the people you call your friends? Dr. Chatman's account of her individual journey allows us to appreciate the differences we all have (and the commonalities we share) now more than ever.

Her story is one that inspires, encourages, and reaffirms the reader who may feel like being an introvert makes it impossible to overcome daily challenges. I know you will be uplifted and walk away being able to see that healing can be yours too. Dr. Chatman is one of my best friends, turned sister. I've been blessed to have her in my life during some trying times and I've walked alongside her as she navigated through life never giving up.

I am an extrovert. Through both tears and laughter, Dr. Chatman and I have both healed and built a long-lasting relationship that is sound and solid. But I had to learn that it was okay for her to take her time to respond. I had to learn that sometimes I may need to contact her first. I had to learn how to love her and care for her because she was learning the same thing about herself as she gained more knowledge about what it means to be an introvert.

We are all created on purpose for a purpose. Sometimes we have barriers that may delay our progress in life, but the key is **not to give up.** Seek professional advice and surround yourself with people who care for you and love you enough to learn and grow with you as you truly find yourself.

So, grab your favorite drink and snack or curl up with a blanket as Dr. Chatman's story of healing and friendship unfolds through the pages of this book. She will allow you to see that "all lives are precious," pointing out a simple, but profound, fact "that there is purpose in pain and there are lessons in the journey." Embrace the pain and every lesson to be a better version of yourself.

You owe it to YOURSELF first.

Sonya M. Sessoms, MBA, MDiv
Pastor: Sound of Worship Center
Author: "How I Faithed it Over"
IG: @iamsonyasessoms
FB: I Am Sonya Sessoms

Preface

I cannot tell you how many times someone has told me that I need to write a book. Not only did I not feel worthy or my life interesting enough to share in a book, but the introvert in me also fights against being in the spotlight. However, God always pushes me beyond my comfort level.

In 2020, I was asked to participate in a panel during a women's ministry event at my new church. I knew that it was an assignment from God because I had only been there about 6 weeks or so, didn't know the minister who asked me to participate, and hadn't said much at church other than "Hi" and "Bye," but she said that God told her I had something to share. So even though I had some self-doubting thoughts like, "What do I have to share? Why would she ask me?" I went to God and asked Him what He wanted me to share.

He prompted me to pull out my journal, so during the panel, I shared some excerpts from it. After the event, a woman walked up to me and told me that morning she was contemplating suicide, and my transparency gave her the courage to get prayer, which she did. We also exchanged phone numbers, and I checked on her regularly.

I'd like to say that right after that confirmation that I started writing, but I didn't. I procrastinated and made excuses... dodging my assignment. Then, in 2021, I participated in a colleague's dissertation study. After the interview, he shut off the recorder and said, "I need you to write a book immediately." I laughed and a day or so later, I saw a *Finish That Book,* a 90-day book writing challenge facilitated by Coach Joy Morgan, and knew that it was time.

My prayer for you, as you read this book, is that you will always know and feel that you are NEVER ALONE. Help is a phone call or text message away. Your life is important and has a purpose. Whatever you are going through won't last forever. Just keep pushing!

Chapter 1

The Discovery

It was 2015, I was 43 years old, and there I was sitting in the marriage counselor/family therapist's office ALONE. My husband at the time had decided (again) that he wasn't going back to counseling.

I was telling her about my mood swings, about the physical toll it seemed to take on my mind and body when I engaged in a lot of social activity and meetings, how sometimes I could not get out of the bed, and how I seemed to need alone time and sleep in a way that seemed unusual, but for the sake of my blended family and marriage, I had to force myself to do things that I physically and mentally didn't have the capacity to do. She started asking those probing questions that counselors tend to ask about my childhood, my job, church activities, family, work relationships, etc. Then, she said something like "Christal, I imagine that it's very difficult for you to push yourself to engage in social activity." I said "Yes. Sometimes, I feel like I'm depressed, and people have always talked about my mood swings." She said, "Christal, you are not depressed, and you are not moody. You are an introvert."

I AM AN INTROVERT.

My mind started spinning. Introvert? I'm not shy. (I said that out loud to her.) Then she started explaining what it meant to be an introvert. While extroverts tend to "recharge" their energy by being around other people, introverts do so from alone time (and sometimes sleep), and absolutely must have "me time." To be honest, I don't recall the rest of our conversation.

My entire life flashed before my eyes.

- The large family gatherings I would quietly exit, feeling exhausted, find a quiet place, and go to sleep. My family still talks about how they would be looking for me and would find me in some room asleep.
- The feelings that I have about attending social gatherings at church, work, or a friend's special event where I have to look around and find someone to sit with or sit at an empty table and wait for them to find me when I would rather be home and chilling in my bed.
- The occasions when I would leave the room or find something else to do at the beginning of an ice breaker activity.
- When a friend comes to visit, after an hour or so, I am all talked out.
- Every time I entered the school lunchroom (elementary, junior high and high school) I would get my lunch, scan the

room for a place to sit, and usually opt to sit alone until a friend joined me.
- When I didn't answer the phone but later responded via text because I just didn't feel like having a verbal conversation.
- During "greet your neighbor" time at church I would do that for about 30 seconds and then fiddle in my handbag to avoid awkward eye contact or forced hugging.
- The moments when my extremely extroverted son would engage a stranger in conversation during vacation, and I would marvel at how he did that with such ease. Then I would cringe inside knowing at some point I would have to make small talk with them too.
- The displeasure I feel when my hubby walks into the room and hands me the phone to talk to someone I wasn't planning to talk to about a business idea or to network.
- Speaking of networking events... enough said!

- The time I was on jury duty and felt like a misfit because I was the only person not engaging in unnecessary, quiet-filling chit-chat and someone asked me why I wasn't talking.
- Why I found it so difficult to sit in a physical classroom as a student and only took online courses, but I love teaching.
- Why I arrive just in time for the meeting to start so that I can avoid small talk. If I arrive too early, I will sit in my car, outside, or in a lobby.

Please don't get me wrong, I love people. I am friendly, but just usually not a proactive talker with people I don't know. I love to joke and have fun. I manage and lead teams effectively. In most cases, people never believe that I'm an introvert because I push beyond that part of myself to engage in a healthy personal, professional, and spiritual life.

However, there are times and social situations where I just don't want to or when I've had back-to-back meetings all day, email requests, and phone calls, and it sends me into what I call an "introvert meltdown" where I just need quiet time for an hour or two. It's hard to explain but I have heard other introverts say, "I have peopled enough for the day."

What I do know is that after 43 years of life, I finally had a context for accepting so many experiences and emotions in my life that I didn't realize I needed to better understand. I left her office with a sense of self-discovery that I cannot adequately describe. I spent days after that researching what it meant to be an introvert and how introverts tend to "show up" when they are in relationships. The Dictionary by Merriam-Webster definition of an introvert is "a person whose personality is characterized by introversion: a typically reserved or quiet person who tends to be introspective and enjoys spending time alone." The term "introversion" was developed by Carl Jung, who suggested that introverts prefer the safety of their own mental life than the external activities of extroverts. Introverts tend to regain energy during times of reflection and rest, and tend to be drained of energy in social situations.

Psychology Today online has a lot of useful information about introverts.[1] For example, introverts:

- Enjoy quiet and solitary experiences
- Are not shy or lonely
- Enjoy one-on-one situations in peaceful settings... crowded parties are equivalent to torture
- Have a low tolerance for small talk
- Be highly attuned to personal interactions
- Can make excellent leaders as they don't tend to need social approval, but will rely on careful analysis and personal values
- Tend to have one or two close friends
- Can be labeled as aloof or standoffish
- Tend to be very observant

- Are not broken and don't need to be fixed.

In a blog post titled, *Understanding Introverts: Being Quiet is Not a Defect* by Beverly Flaxington,[2] she writes about how America tends to favor extroverts over introverts. People frequently ask introverts why they are so quiet. Rewards and acknowledgments are given more to extroverts because they tend to stand out more. The push to network and engage in social media to promote yourself is a scenario in which extroverts can thrive but may be too much for introverts. All of this can lead an introvert to think, "What is wrong with me and how could I possibly have a successful relationship?"

The truth is that we're all different and no matter what friendships or relationships we're in, we must teach the other person about ourselves, so we are able to learn how to be in a relationship characterized by mutual respect and understanding. It's really important for me to note that these are my experiences and may not be the experiences of other introverts. I've also learned that perhaps I had a little social anxiety that played a role in my experiences as well, which is different from being an introvert but is something that many introverts also have. After I had done a lot of online research on being an introvert, I began to feel like being an introvert was a flaw and it made me a little uneasy. "Who in the world would care enough about me to take time to understand what it would take to be my friend or husband?" Over the next couple of months, I had to fortify myself by learning why God made me this way.

It's usually easier when we find someone that we can identify with who has a similar issue or trait. So, when I thought about someone in the Bible who could have been an introvert, I immediately thought of Moses.

Moses was a great leader who was seemingly an introvert. He was afraid of public speaking and had self-doubt that is typically seen in introverts. In Exodus chapters 3 and 4, God gives Moses instructions to go to Egypt and tell Pharaoh to free the Israelites from slavery. Moses questioned his worth and responded by asking God who he is to go to Pharaoh to deliver that message. God reminded him that wasn't about who Moses was, but about who God is and that Moses was to go and tell Pharaoh that God said it.

Typical of an introvert, Moses replied, "And what do I do if they don't believe or listen to me?" God gave Moses two different miracles that he could perform as signs that God sent him. Moses still had questions and doubts; he told God about his speech impediment as if God didn't know about that and hadn't purposely made him that way.

The Lord was frustrated with Moses, and He reminded him that He is the one who created the body. God commanded Moses to go to Pharaoh and reassured him that God's presence and power were with him. After all of that, Moses still asked God to send someone else. So, He gave Moses' brother Aaron the assignment to speak for Moses, while Moses had the staff to perform the signs. Moses was clearly afraid to be the voice of God that challenged Pharaoh and led the Israelites out of Egypt.

I encourage you to read the full story for yourself in Exodus chapters 1-20. Ultimately, God's plan was accomplished, but there were hurdles. Oftentimes, I wonder what would have happened if Moses had set aside his self doubt and given the message alone as God intended. I'm sure Pharaoh and the Israelites probably knew or heard about his speech impediment, but how much more powerful and direct would it have been to see Moses' confidence in God displayed despite his perceived flaw.

On a related note, I want to remind you that **only you** can tell your story or lead the assignment given to you; flaws, self-doubt, and all. However, if you refuse or make excuses, God will raise up someone else. If you have something you're supposed to be doing, such as starting a business, leading a ministry, or even writing a book, be obedient and get it done!

Speaking of perceived flaws, what, if anything, does the Bible say about being an introvert? Psalm 139:13-16 tells us that God knew us when we were in our mother's womb. His eyes could see our unformed bodies and every one of our days were ordained by Him while we were being formed. We are fearfully and wonderfully made!

Consider this: God purposely created us with unique differences that we sometimes view as imperfections and flaws that need to be corrected, but He intentionally added these to our physical, mental, and emotional makeup. He is the Potter and we are the clay... the works of His hands (Isaiah 64:8). The Bible reminds us that "God created mankind in his own image, in the image of God he created them; male and female he created them" (Genesis 1:27 NIV).

Have you ever thought that your perceived flaws were mistakes meant to cause you pain, or did you believe they were part of a larger plan? Maybe it's a health issue, a physical attribute, or a personality trait that you don't like. One of my favorite scriptures that has always gotten me through feelings of insecurity is Jeremiah 29:11, "For I know the plans I have for you," declares the Lord, "plans to prosper you and not to harm you, plans to give you hope and a future."

First Corinthians 12 provides the perspective that God has given us various spiritual gifts, and each one is important in the body of Christ. One part of the body cannot tell another part of the body that it isn't needed, nor should one part of the body consider itself unworthy because another part of the body seems more important. God created us just as He meant us to be.

Every perceived flaw, every difference, and every gift God has given to us is meant to serve a divine purpose.

Take a moment to think about the flaw or uniqueness that comes to mind through that lens. How does that change your perspective on that attribute?

My "aha" moments:

1. You can be a Christian and see a therapist.
2. True healing comes through self-discovery.
3. There is nothing wrong with being an introvert or an extrovert, or anything in between.
4. If you frequently interact with someone who has opposite personality traits from yours, please take the time to learn how best to be in a personal or professional relationship with them.

Chapter 2

My Journey

I AM AN INTROVERT.

Here's a little background about me that may put my response to trauma, healing, and perseverance into perspective. Looking back on it, I realize how much of these experiences impacted how I view myself today. I was raised in Philly, PA along with my brother who is 9 years younger than me. My parents were high school sweethearts and have been married for over 50 years.

I went to a Montessori school from kindergarten to third grade. Each day, our assignments were on the blackboard and we could work on them in whatever order we wanted. We asked the teacher questions, when necessary, but each student worked at their own pace for reading, math, and language studies. Almost every week, our class would make lunch together. We had a budget, a list of ingredients, and would walk to the grocery store together to purchase our items before heading back to school to make our class lunch (hoagies, spaghetti, etc.). We took frequent field trips and had several pets in the class that we were allowed to take home. Those memories are priceless!

Then, I went to a Christian school from 4th grade to 8th grade. This school was modeled toward the standard educational system with lessons taught by teachers, exams, report cards, etc. This school established the roots of my spiritual foundation and I accepted Christ into my life. My school had annual retreats, concerts, field days, visits to our teachers' homes, and even street evangelism. Through that journey, I was also able to lead my mom to Christ.

After my mom got saved, we joined a local neighborhood church. I sang on the youth choir and went to youth group activities regularly. I am blessed to say that I am still in touch with and friends with many of my classmates from those years. As I think back, I really don't recall feelings of being an introvert before my teenage years.

In 9th grade, I spent one year at my neighborhood public school. Once I started attending a large public school, I started feeling like something was "different" about my personality. With my prior private school education, I was further along academically than many of my peers, so even though I didn't talk much, I was noticed by my teachers very quickly. I took a typing class and learned how to type 90 words per minute, which became my saving grace in many ways.

Being an introvert, the thought of finding a place for lunch gave me a level of anxiety that I can't really describe, not to mention how lame I felt sitting at a huge table by myself. For me, it was like walking into a crowd at a stadium and trying to find a friend. The crazy thing is that I had a lot of "friends" at school because I was a nice person and friendly, yet I still felt alone. As a result, I always felt like schools should create quiet lunch spaces for kids with social anxieties or those who want to study so that they can avoid the whole lunchroom pressure of finding a seat or sitting alone.

With my academic performance and typing skills, I was able to escape the lunch situation because I graded papers for some of the teachers and I typed up their exams and reports. I also worked in the school office. The teachers got some extra help for which they paid me, and I didn't have to experience the lunchroom. It was a win-win. The icing on the cake was that I was asked to represent the school in the Philadelphia School District spelling bee and finished as a runner-up. I also graduated as salutatorian and gave a speech for graduation. As I reflect on those two events, I don't recall feeling the nervousness or the "shyness" I often felt in other social situations.

In the summer of my freshman year of high school, my mom was tired of seeing me sit around the house watching TV. So, she made me volunteer unpaid to work with her friend who was the Director of Financial Aid at Antioch University in Philadelphia. My mom had worked there before and the staff there knew me well from the days when I would hang out with my mom at her job helping her record student payments on their paper ledger cards. After about a week of volunteering there, several of the students who were really impressed with my work ethic and friendliness petitioned the school director to hire me, and he did just that. The staff there took care of me like I was one of their children. They made sure that I ate, checked on me throughout the day, and made sure I made it home safely in the evenings.

Within a few months, the director left, and I was running the office. I had to learn the financial aid management system, how to process all types of financial aid, and I gave direction to the administrative assistant who was three times my age. Even though I was a high school student, I knew that I was doing way more work than I was being paid for, so I asked for a raise and got it. After several months, a new director was hired. She was amazed that I had been running the entire office part-time after school and that everything was in great shape. She taught me more about higher-level aspects of financial aid and I taught her how to use the financial aid management system. So, my financial aid career began when I was only 15 years old.

In Fall 1986, I started attending Philadelphia's Central High School. (I am proud to say "248" at any moment! If you're a Lancer, then you already know.) Central was a vibrant, fun, close-knit environment. While I made lifelong friendships and enjoyed my time there, I became acutely aware that my social experiences were very different from those of my classmates. While they were going to games, attending parties, joining high school sports teams, cheerleading, and other school groups, I was either going to work or going home. I took a computer science class, and the teacher was physically disabled so he had a teaching assistant. I can't really remember when or how, but the assistant and I developed a little sister/big sister relationship. We usually had lunch together and talked, and I rarely had to deal with the anxiety of the lunchroom.

It's crazy to reflect on this time in my life because I knew a lot of people in high school. We talked on the phone, talked in the hallway, and hung out at each other's homes, but I could not engage in large group settings. If there was an overwhelming amount of activity, I would go home, fall asleep, and not wake up until the next morning. When I look at pictures on social media from high school, I'm not present in any of them except one or two moments in the hallway, next to a locker with a friend or two. Sometimes I feel like I missed out on a lot of the high school experience, but even if I had known why I felt the way I felt, I don't think anything would be different.

After graduating from high school, I went to Temple University and lived in an off-campus apartment because I couldn't imagine living in a dorm and sharing a room with someone... talk about an introvert's nightmare! I went to class then I went home or to work. Since I had so much financial aid experience, I was able to go into the financial aid office, tell them about my work experience, and get hired right on the spot to work on the Health Sciences Campus where I supervised other student workers, trained staff, and processed financial aid for the students. While I didn't graduate from Temple, I completed my bachelor's degree at Chestnut Hill College, master's degree at DeVry University/ Keller Graduate School of Management, and at my mom's suggestion that I "might as well go ahead and get my doctoral degree," I obtained my Doctor of Business Administration degree at the University of Phoenix after 10 years of hard work.

Over the years, within the church, I was a Youth Director, Community Outreach Director, and Church Administrator. I have worked at various colleges as Director of Financial Aid, Bursar, Dean, Director of Financial Services, and Adjunct Faculty. As I reflect on my life, especially my doctoral journey, perseverance has always been a constant factor though I didn't always understand why I had to go through some of the things that I experienced. The Merriam-Webster definition of "perseverance" is the "continued effort to do or achieve something despite difficulties, failure, or opposition: the action or condition or an instance of persevering: steadfastness."

Even writing this book, I was met with many obstacles. I'm not sure if the enemy was trying to distract me, if God was giving me another testimony, or if I was making myself sick just thinking about writing a book, but from the moment I accepted the challenge, the obstacles appeared.

During a routine physical exam, I was diagnosed with a couple of health issues and for months, I went through a trial-and-error process with my doctor trying to find the right medication. In the meantime, I suffered from extreme fatigue, nausea, and headaches. Sometimes I spent days in bed. Then, hubby and I went on a getaway to the Dominican Republic, and on the second day, I got food poisoning that had me debilitatingly sick for 3 weeks. On the day that I decided to push myself to finish the book, I scheduled a hair appointment and photoshoot and woke up the next morning with another illness that lasted two weeks. I have never had this many occurrences of sickness in my entire life. All of this happened while I was concurrently juggling work priorities and family responsibilities, but I promised myself and God that I would finish this book, so I did.

However, I had questions about why I had to go through all of that. As with many of my life's experiences, I try to find the answers in the Word. The following scriptures are ones that I believe really shed some light on the "why" of it all. Romans 5:1-5 says, "Therefore, since we have been justified through faith, we have peace with God through our Lord Jesus Christ, through whom we have gained access by faith into this grace in which we now stand. And we boast in the hope of the glory of God. Not only so, but we also glory in our sufferings, because we know that suffering produces perseverance; perseverance, character; and character, hope. And hope does not put us to shame, because God's love has been poured out into our hearts through the Holy Spirit, who has been given to us?"

James 1:2-4 says, "Consider it pure joy, my brothers and sisters, whenever you face trials of many kinds because you know that the testing of your faith produces perseverance. Let perseverance finish its work so that you may be mature and complete, not lacking anything." When I was in the doctorate program, I sometimes felt like a wandering Israelite.[1] I watched others in my cohort graduate while I was still in the program. Some of the delays had to do with life issues, such as the pressures of starting a new job, balancing work, family, and school, and issues with the dissertation process. However, the truth is that most of the delays were because I was busy complaining and procrastinating about being so tired that the process didn't seem as easy for me as it seemed for others.

I kept trying to remind myself of what one of my professors said early on in the program, which was that obtaining a doctorate degree has very little to do with intelligence and everything to do with perseverance and humility. In summary, suffering and the testing of your faith produces perseverance and perseverance produces character, maturity, and completion so that you will not lack anything! If you learn how to persevere through challenges, you will succeed, you will learn how to get through future challenges, and you will lack NOTHING.

Time to take a pause... Shout out to my mom for pushing me into a career, leadership, a terminal degree, and ministry! Shout out to my dad for being my biggest cheerleader and supporter in everything. I still remember leading the Outreach Team as we were holding a back-to-school community event that drew close to 1,000 people and looking up to see my dad walking around.

Speaking of parenthood, I had my son, Brent, a couple of weeks after I completed my undergraduate degree when I was 29 years old. From the time he was a toddler, it was clear that there was an anointing on his life. If you have ever met him, then you know! Ultimately, it's up to him to share his story at the appointed time in his life so I won't go into details, but there is always a cost for the anointing. My baby has been through a lot, and as his mom, the cost and favor associated with his anointing were on my life too. There were times that I cried feeling like I wasn't a good enough parent for him, unsure of how to raise him, and hurting from the pain he's experienced. However, every day has been well worth it. I am so honored to journey alongside him, guiding him, advising him, pushing him, correcting him, and best of all…

loving him with all that is in me even when it was tough love.

Parents, your words, behavior, support, and influence can totally push your children toward purpose and destiny.

Chapter 3

Where Was God?

I AM AN INTROVERT.

Some of us treat our friendships like a credit line. The finance company gives you a credit line where purchases, charges, and cash advances reduce your available balance, and when payments are made, the credit line is restored and available for future withdrawals. Unconsciously, we can view our friendships like that. Talking about problems, calling for help, or borrowing money are like charges against the credit line, and listening, helping, giving advice, and loaning money to a friend are like making payments to restore the credit line.

Imagine not speaking with your friend in 6 months and calling to talk about a problem or to borrow money for food. Many of us would probably not do that because we haven't made any payments on the friendship credit line. We'd also probably feel like we're being used if our friend hadn't called in 6 months and out of the blue called to ask for something. Somewhere in the recesses of our minds, we can think of our friendships as transactional, when you are asking yourself, "When was the last time I talked to her? How is she going to feel if I call after all this time just to ask for help or talk about my problems?"

Recently, I had a conversation with a longtime friend that went something like this:

> *Friend: I was going through X and really wanted to call you because I knew you*

went through something similar and would totally understand.

Me: I had no idea you were dealing with X. Why didn't you call me?

Friend: I didn't want to burden you with my problems. I know you have your own stuff going on.

Me: Girl, I love you. You know that you can call me any time day or night. I would have wanted to be there for you while you were dealing with X.

Friend: I know.

Have you ever had a similar conversation or failed to call a friend for help because you didn't want to burden him/her? The truth is that true friendship is not transactional, it's transformational. We support one another without judgment, talk about the good and the bad, and grow and develop personally, professionally, and spiritually no matter whether the friendship is for a reason, season, or a lifetime.

People come into your life for a reason, a season, or a lifetime.

When someone is in your life for a REASON, it is usually to meet a need you have expressed or just felt. They have come to assist you through a hard time, to provide you with guidance and support, to aid you physically, emotionally, or spiritually. Then, suddenly, the person disappears from your life. Your need has been met; their work is done.

Some people come into your life for a SEASON, because your turn has come to share or grow or give back. They bring you an experience of peace or make you laugh. They give you great joy. Believe it; it is real. But only for a season.

LIFETIME relationships teach you lifetime lessons—things you must build upon to have a solid emotional foundation. Your job is to accept the lesson, love the person and put what you have learned to use in all your other relationships.

Think about the people in your life over the years. Whether they were there for a reason, a season, or a lifetime, accept them and treasure them for however long they were meant to be part of your life.

And when they are gone, be thankful for the gifts you received from them when they were here—for a reason, a season, or a lifetime. ~~Brian A. "Drew" Chalker

Recognizing that friendships can be for a reason, season, or a lifetime, I truly pray that your friendships are not "credit line friendships," that you nurture and invest time to check on the well-being of your friends and pray for them, especially the "strong and quiet ones." I pray that you are able to recognize and be thankful for the gift of all friendships no matter how long they have lasted. All my life, I've usually had about one or two close friends with whom I felt comfortable talking to about my "stuff." I've been burned before by people I thought were my friends but betrayed my trust. I learned some difficult lessons, especially for an introvert who does not make friends easily, but I survived, persevered, and learned.

When I was about 43 years old, I had five really close church friends, which was very unusual for me and I couldn't really understand or explain it. In hindsight, it was almost as if God knew what was about to happen and who I needed to surround me to help me push past my introverted tendencies and deflections instead of seeking help. Ok, who am I kidding? Of course, God knew. He always knows.

Each friendship started under a different circumstance, but all of them started in church. I've weathered storms with each one, we've laughed together, cried together, helped one another financially when needed, prayed for one another, vacationed together, frequently dined together, attended each other's weddings, watched our children grow up, and supported one another through relationship issues. They are family to me.

So, in November 2015, my first husband and I decided to separate after almost 5 years of marriage. On that day, I still went to church. I sent my son inside, sat in the car, and started crying. One of the mothers of the church was walking by and saw me in the car crying. She got into the car and proceeded to listen, talk, encourage, and pray for me. Then, she told me to get myself together and she'd see me inside. So I did.

I remember one of my friends texting me about something. I don't remember what it was, but I remember texting "I ended my marriage today." Who does that during church? Clearly, I was in some level of shock. I sat in church, stoically. I might have wiped away a tear or two, but no one knew the major life event that had taken place moments earlier.

I went back to the counselor to let her know what had happened, and she told me that she was expecting this outcome. We spent some time talking about my next steps. I thought that I had it all together, but I also thought the marriage was going to last forever. I had prayed for God to fix it and felt like He didn't answer me but later realized that He absolutely answered me. I'll just let that sit there for a minute.

Sometimes, God's answer is "Go."

Still, there was a break deep down in my soul. While I had resigned myself to where this was headed, there was still an enormous amount of pain at the loss of the marriage despite the circumstances. My emotional state and thoughts were about how I felt about myself and God. I thought I hadn't done enough, hadn't prayed enough, hadn't had enough faith, hadn't submitted enough, hadn't… hadn't… hadn't….

I felt like I'd wasted years of my life. I was embarrassed. I was hurt. I felt like a failure. I felt like a bad Christian.

My mind was spinning with thoughts. Ephesians 6:12 says, "For our struggle is not against flesh and blood, but against the rulers, against the authorities, against the powers of this dark world and against the spiritual forces of evil in the heavenly realms." In the book, "Battlefield of the Mind" by Joyce Meyer, which I highly recommend, she talks about the strongholds on our minds that the enemy tries to set up to place us in bondage through our thoughts and she explains the importance of gaining control of our thoughts.

"He (the enemy/devil) begins by bombarding our mind with a clearly devised pattern of little nagging thoughts, suspicions, doubts, fears, wonderings, reasonings, and theories. He moves slowly and cautiously (after all, well-laid plans take time). Remember, he has a strategy for his warfare. He has studied us for a long time. He knows what we like and what we don't like. He knows our insecurities, our weaknesses, and our fears. He knows what bothers us the most."[4] I kept thinking, why did He allow this to happen to me? Where was He?

When I couldn't bring myself to pray because I didn't have the words, I would write out my thoughts and prayers in a journal:

Excerpt #1
God, I ended the marriage. I am heartbroken and hurt beyond words, but I know my worth... God, heal my heart, protect my mind, cover my family, and fulfill your purpose in me... God, I trust you to work this out for my good.

Excerpt #2
God, it's been a week... Last week, Pastor preached that there is purpose in our pain. What's the purpose in this? What was the purpose in him finding me for it to end this way? Why? Why?

I am so hurt, angry, embarrassed. Yet, I still have to stand and press forward when I really want to just give up. What's next? What possible good could come from this? What did I do or fail to do to deserve this? I am so tired of crying...

I keep listening to music to try to praise my way through and fill my spirit with you. I keep trying to think of comforting scriptures. When will it stop hurting?

Anyway, I guess you're probably tired of my pity party. So, I ask that you heal my heart, protect my mind, provide for my family, and wrap your arms around me so that I can receive your peace, comfort, and love. God your will be done in this situation.

Excerpt #3
God, this doesn't seem real. Why did this happen? What is the purpose? These are the questions floating around in my mind.

Anyway, I trust you to bring me through this. Your will be done. There will be purpose in my pain.

Excerpt #4
God this last week has now brought me to a place where this doesn't feel real. I keep hoping I will wake up and everything will go back to the

way it was. I know you have plan. I know that you won't put more on me than I can bear. I know that I can do all things through Christ. I know and have heard all of the usual scriptures, but I need you and your presence. This feels like more than I can bear. I trust you to provide, protect, love, and comfort. Please remove the uncertainty.

When I was home, I cried, but always hid in my bedroom or bathroom so that my son wouldn't see me cry. I was worried about his well-being more than mine. I was always checking on him to make sure that he was adjusting to the change in the household, and that he wouldn't have cause to worry about me. I later learned that he was worried about me even though I tried to shield him from my pain.

When I went out to work or church, I put on my mask and said, "I'm OK." I always kept Visine with me because tears would unexpectedly fall when I wasn't even thinking about it or was still for too long. Thank God for an office with a door because that door stayed shut often. Each one of my friends knew about what happened and lovingly accepted my introverted tendencies. They were on an earthly assignment from God to save my life.

Friend 1 would call me a few times per week, and whenever I called her, she would answer. She would let me talk and cry for a little bit, encourage me, and then say, "OK. You've cried enough for now. Let's talk about something else." It was just what I needed to get it out and focus on all the other good things in my life.

Friend 2 would also call me regularly, check to see if I needed anything, and would sometimes take my son to church or events when I just didn't have the emotional energy to go. She would frequently offer to bring me a can of soup, as an inside joke. Little did I know that she would ultimately save my life.

Friend 3 would call or text me DAILY. I tear up just thinking about the level of relationship that would prompt someone to check on another person every single day. On days when I wouldn't respond, I would get a text that said "OK. I haven't heard from you in a couple of days, or I haven't seen you in church in a few Sundays. Don't make me drive over to your house." That right there is enough to make an introvert respond quickly! So, I would.

Friend 4 also called and checked on me regularly. One day, I called her because I really didn't want to be alone. She was out and about, asked me how I was doing, and I told her that I wasn't doing well. She stopped everything and came right over. For the entire time she was at my house, she held me and let me weep and cry. Sometimes, you just need someone to hold you and let you know that everything is gonna be alright. I am eternally grateful for that moment with her.

Friend 5 is my funny, sensitive, ride-or-die friend, who lives out of state but would hop on a plane if needed, to check on me. She would call to check on me, and after the venting and tears, we'd end up laughing hysterically. That's how we always roll.

Despite having these wonderful women in my life, I still found myself pretending to the outside world that I was "OK".

Chapter 4

I'm OK

I AM AN INTROVERT.

"I'm OK." It's not an introvert-specific phrase, but it must be one of the most common and deflective responses we say use to avoid talking about what's really going on in our lives. It's a figurative mask in the form of a phrase. I always imagine that it looks like those fake smiling theater masks you see on the playbills.

Why? Where does come from? Where did we learn to hide our feelings? I'm sure most of us can recall moments throughout childhood where these roots began.

Emotional tears have health benefits. In a peer-reviewed article by Lana Burgess (2017) titled, *Eight benefits of crying: Why it's good to shed a few tears*,[5] she writes that crying is a natural response to our emotions. We cry when we're sad, hurt, happy, frustrated, stressed, or grieving. While we may try to hide or suppress tears as a sign of weakness, here are eight benefits found in research.

1. Crying helps to soothe, regulate our emotions, and reduce feelings of distress.

2. Crying is a visible signal to others that we need help and may prompt them to provide needed support.

3. Crying releases oxytocin and endorphins that ease physical pain.

4. Crying makes us feel better and the release of those chemicals can improve our mood.

5. Crying releases stress hormones through the tears, which may reduce stress.

6. Crying has a sleep-inducing effect. Sidenote: After a good cry, I sleep like nobody's business!

7. Crying kills bacteria and cleans the eyes.

8. Crying keeps the eyes moist and helps keep vision clear.

Well, if girls and boys, men and women can cry, why isn't it OK for us to cry?

For some of us, it may be that we don't want the attention of people looking at us and wondering what's wrong even though we may need the attention. I found these gems in another article/blog called "6 Reasons Why Introverts Hide Their Feelings." [6]

1. Introverts don't want to upset people.

2. Introverts don't trust others (yet).

3. Introverts tend to be modest and may believe that no one is interested in their thoughts.

4. Introverts may not share if they aren't asked the right questions.

5. Introverts need to time process their feelings before they share them.

6. Introverts do not want to be the center of attention.

Outside of the introvert-specific reasons for hiding emotions cited above, could it also be that we are uncomfortable with how our tears make others feel when they see us cry? Is there an unspoken obligation that puts us out or makes us feel like we're burdening someone with our tears?

In Psalm 56:8, it is written that God bottles every tear and records them in His record. Can you imagine that level of love, care, and empathy? He would not have created tears or recorded them if they weren't important to us and Him.

Psalm 126:5-7 reads, "Those who sow with tears will reap with songs of joy. Those who go out weeping, carrying seed to sow, will return with songs of joy, carrying sheaves with them." Tears water the seeds that are planted, and joy is the harvest, for "weeping may endure for a night, but joy cometh in the morning" (Psalm 30:5).

God made us beings who can think and feel. Though introverts tend to have a more difficult time expressing emotions openly, all of us have emotions, so it would stand to reason that it's normal to have emotional moments. Perhaps the key is what we do when we're emotional and how long we stay in that emotional place.

It's also important to consider the effect of social media on our perception of reality. Stories and posts on social media are just a snippet of our lives and businesses that we want people to see. It's usually all the good stuff... vacations, new cars, children's milestones, date nights, promotions, conferences, business ventures, and selfies on top of selfies on top of selfies.

All those posts will make you think that everybody's lives are perfect. What you don't see on social media are financial struggles; emotional, verbal, or physical abuse; relationship issues; cheating; our children bullying or being bullied; long hours working on business ideas; all the no's an entrepreneur has received before one yes; family drama; and feelings of doubt, fear, sadness, jealousy, anger, suicide, etc. All we see are masks. We have no idea what struggles people are experiencing.

My church routine has been to put on mask, smile and hug, participate in praise and worship, greet people, take notes during the sermon, and no matter what, do not let one tear fall or the floodgates will open PUBLICLY, and all eyes and minds will be on me wondering what is wrong with me? I cringe a lot at the thought of these things, but people looking at me when I'm emotional is high on the list of things I want to avoid. As I've gotten older and more mature, I care less and less about what people think and am more focused on my healing, peace, and joy.

One Sunday, I gathered the strength to go to church even though I was hanging onto my emotional stability by a thread! I just needed to avoid lingering conversation and those church hugs that could cause the wall that was protecting my emotions from crumbling to pieces. So, I smiled, gave quick hugs, and participated in the service as best I could. I don't think anyone realized how fragile I was.

When I walked past someone who I knew that I could be vulnerable with and trust with my emotions, I also knew that if I gave an inch, I would break down right there, in that hallway, in front of everyone and may not be able to get up. So when she asked how I was doing, in the way that I knew she really wanted to know and really cared, without maintaining full eye contact, I said, "I'm OK." She asked, "Are you sure?" I said "Yup."

I walked away sad and frustrated with myself because I desperately needed to share but was afraid to remove my mask. I was afraid of what people would think if they saw me crying because I just knew they heard about my situation or were making assumptions because I was attending church alone now. I was afraid that if I removed my mask in that moment, I would have a breakdown that would take hours to control.

What I didn't consider is that I might have had the breakthrough that I so desperately needed, and that God wanted me to have it right there in the place that is supposed to be the spiritual hospital for the brokenhearted. Matthew 11:28-29 says, "Come to me, all you who are weary and burdened, and I will give you rest. Take my yoke upon you and learn from me, for I am gentle and humble in heart, and you will find rest for your souls." I was moments away from having the burden of the day lifted and finding rest, but I chose my introverted tendencies, or perhaps it was pride.

How often do we choose pride over healing, pride over resolution, pride over vulnerability, or pride over humility? The Bible has a lot to say about pride. Pride keeps us from hearing from God. Pride keeps us from growing and progressing toward purpose. Pride keeps us from getting healed. Pride creates division. Pride reflects a condescending spirit that is not of God and not God's love. Pride blocks wisdom.

Proverbs 16:18 says, "Pride goes before destruction, a haughty spirit before a fall."

Proverbs 11:2-3 says, "When pride comes,

then comes disgrace, but with humility comes wisdom. The integrity of the upright guides them, but the unfaithful are destroyed by their duplicity."

Proverbs 13:10-11 says, "Where there is strife, there is pride, but wisdom is found in those who take advice."

Proverbs is full of wisdom! Proverbs 12:9 really hit home for me: "Better to be a nobody and yet have a servant than pretend to be somebody and have no food." How much better is it to remove the mask and get help versus wearing the mask and pretending that everything is OK, while you are in pain, hungry, alone, and dying inside?

Perhaps the better, humbler path that leads to healing and growth is Matthew 7:7-12:
Ask, Seek, Knock...
[7] "Ask and it will be given to you; seek and you will find; knock and the door will be opened to you. [8] For everyone who asks receives; the one who seeks finds; and to the one

who knocks, the door will be opened. [9] "Which of you, if your son asks for bread, will give him a stone? [10] Or if he asks for a fish, will give him a snake? [11] If you, then, though you are evil, know how to give good gifts to your children, how much more will your Father in heaven give good gifts to those who ask him! [12] So in everything, do to others what you would have them do to you, for this sums up the Law and the Prophets."

If you need help, ask for it, but be sure your motives are right (James 4:2b-3). The tears cannot be about manipulation or to getting someone on your side or getting what you want. Genuine tears and a cry out to God for help can lead to healing, resolution, or a need being met. Pride leads nowhere. Are you familiar with that saying, "Closed mouths don't get fed?" Well... think about that for a moment.

Our lives depend on some amount of transparency and removal of the masks we wear to hide emotions, needs, and pain from people. Here's the caveat: not everyone is meant or built to carry your burden. So, we must ask God and exercise wisdom even in trying to get help. I learned that the hard way.

In "The Masks That We Wear" by Susan Sparks (2015), she writes that removing masks is necessary for healing. Failing to do so is akin to withholding pieces of ourselves like part of a broken lamp and expecting someone to help put the pieces back together when a few of the pieces are missing.

Take time to think about the reasons you aren't being your authentic self and are wearing a mask. What happened in your life that caused you to put it on? Was it something someone said or did? Was it a traumatic experience? Now, consider what's the worst that could happen if you took off the mask.

> It is OK to not be OK.
> If you put the mask on, you can choose to take it off.

Removing the mask is not easy and without the outpouring of love from my friends, when The Day came, I am not sure I would have had the strength to resist. Just as God was there all the time looking out for me, please trust that He is there all the time watching over and protecting you. Just take a minute to reflect, look around and find Him, or be still and listen for His voice.

Chapter 5

The Day

I AM AN INTROVERT.

Being an introvert, I usually LOVE and NEED to have alone time, but it can also be isolating and quiet, and that is usually the time when the enemy begins to whisper his foolishness into our ears. Remember the scripture, "The thief comes only to steal and kill and destroy; I have come that they may have life, and have it to the full." (John 10:10). During a period of isolation and fasting, the devil tried to get Jesus to throw himself off the highest point of the temple (Matthew 4:5).

I had spent quite a bit of time alone in my thoughts or binge-watching TV and playing games on my phone trying not to think about my circumstances, but that never works. The thoughts always surface, especially in quiet moments. I had cried myself to sleep many nights or found myself crying in the shower. Even wine wasn't enough to quiet my mind.

One Friday evening in December, my son was with his father for the weekend, and I was looking forward to having an empty house, enjoying a glass of wine, and chilling by myself. I really thought that I was OK. I walked in the house, went into the kitchen, and placed the bottle of wine in the fridge. Instead of feeling at ease and relaxed, an overwhelming heaviness fell over me as I stood in the kitchen to the point that I screamed loudly for about 30 seconds just to get it to lift. Then, I heard a voice in my mind, as if someone was whispering in my ear, clearly saying, "You could just end it all while you're here alone, you don't have to feel sad anymore or deal with all of this stuff by yourself single again, and your family will take care of Brent."

I instantly I knew I needed to get someone over to my house immediately, but I couldn't speak. I literally could not talk. I was crying and I felt like my voice was being oppressed and suppressed. I could not utter a word. I called one of my friends. She answered, and said something like "Hey, girl." I didn't respond. She said, "Are you OK?" I didn't respond. She said, "I'm on my way."

I have no idea where she was when I called or how long it would take her to get to me. Through a fog of tears, I walked to the door, unlocked it, and opened it slightly. I sat down on the couch and let the tears fall. I don't recall any specific thoughts on my mind other than realizing that I was in a bad place when the enemy was in my home speaking to me, and for a few seconds, I thought about how I might end my life by taking sleeping pills.

At some point, my friend walked in, looked at me, said "Oh, Christal." All I wanted was for her to grab me, hold me and let me cry. However, she did something that I didn't understand. And at that moment, it angered me. She sat in a chair on the other side of the room and started praying. She didn't hug me, talk to me, or tell me everything was going to be OK. I was in and out of reality but remember having moments when I would think, "Why isn't she holding me and comforting me?" She was doing something for me that I could not do for myself. She was interceding for me. She was praying for me. I didn't need a hug. I didn't need a "woo-woo" moment. I didn't need a human touch. I needed a touch from God.

By the way, she didn't know what happened before she arrived. She had no idea what the enemy had said to me, but she saw something that let her know that I needed God.

So, I laid on the couch, crying, wailing, and uttering loud groans from my soul that in my life, I had never felt or verbalized or heard before. I literally felt the groans coming from in my depths of heart. I knew that God understood everything my spirit was communicating that my mind could not put into words.

Have you ever lost your voice? Have you ever been at a loss for words and not known what to pray? Sometimes, our souls are so broken that we can't find the words or may lose the ability to speak.

Romans 8:24-28 states, "For in this hope we were saved. But hope that is seen is no hope at all. Who hopes for what they already have? But if we hope for what we do not yet have, we wait for it patiently. In the same way, the Spirit helps us in our weaknesses. We do not know what we ought to pray for, but the Spirit himself intercedes for us through wordless groans. And he who searches our hearts knows the mind of the Spirit because the Spirit intercedes for God's people in accordance with the will of God. And we know that in all things God works for the good of those who love him, who have been called according to his purpose."

Thank God that I had a friend in my life who knew the power of prayer, what I needed at that moment, and could verbalize what my mind, heart, soul, and mouth could not. My friend prayed for me for what seemed like hours, and she continued praying until my weeping and groaning stopped. A peace washed over me that I'm not sure I've ever experienced before, and I knew that it was God's peace that passes all understanding which would guard my heart and mind in Christ Jesus (Philippians 4:6). I knew that I wanted to live!

After I finished wiping the tears from my face, shirt, and couch, there was a huge pile of tissues leftover. She offered to make me some tea, and get me some food or water, but her work was done. She had invoked the heavenly realm on my behalf. I assured her that I was fine and thanked her for coming. I hugged her and she left.

Exhausted, I showered, ate something, and climbed into the bed. I'd like to tell you that I was 100% well after that encounter, but it took a little more time for me to get out of the bed, literally and figuratively.

Please take note that my friend NEVER asked me what happened or what was wrong. It was months before I shared with her what had happened on that day and what she had saved me from doing. The singer/songwriter J. Moss has a song called "The Prayers of the Righteous," which I absolutely love…

Can anybody out there pray for me?
Without even knowin' what I need.
Can anybody pray for me, the prayers of the
Righteous.

Can anybody out there pray for me?
Without even knowin' a whole lot about me?
Can anybody pray where the prayers don't
cease, the prayers of the Righteous

The truth is that we don't need to know what's going on with a person to pray for them. Sometimes we feel that we need to know what specifically to include in our prayers, but that's not true. God knows what the person needs. All we need to do is pray!

We are called to carry one another's burdens (Galatians 6:2), which means lifting the weight off someone's shoulders; figuratively and spiritually speaking. That comes in many forms: prayer, wellness checks via phone or text, cooking a meal, sending a "thinking of you" card, an invitation to a restaurant for coffee or a meal, etc. When you know that someone has gone through a difficult time, such as sickness, divorce, separation, death, or loss of job, we have a responsibility as believers to do regular check-ins, pray in case they can't, and be available when needed.

What if your phone call or text is the one that keeps the person encouraged or prevents them from committing suicide? It only takes a moment to change the trajectory of someone's life.

If you do not get anything else from this

book, please take this with you. Do not avoid people who you know are going through difficult times, especially in the church, which is meant to be a place of love and healing. It may make you uncomfortable but push past those feelings and care enough about the person's wellbeing to ask how they are doing, if they need anything, and remind them that you're praying for them.

One of the most isolating and hurtful aspects of this time of my life was that people that I served with in ministry for 5-10 years, who saw me in church on Sundays, had attended our wedding, or participated in the monthly marriage ministry with us, knew that our marriage had ended yet walked past me every Sunday and never asked me how I was doing. Except for two very special ladies who would message me periodically on social media, most never acknowledged that I went through a major life event and may be hurting. In hindsight, I realize they may not have even known what to say because we tend to focus on happy marriages in church and not much on healing and recovery after divorce.

On the Sundays when I could press forward to go to church, I was so uncomfortable no longer being a church leader (by choice because I needed to heal), uncomfortable looking at the other married couples, uncomfortable listening to sermons about marriage and how people are too quick to divorce, uncomfortable knowing that people knew I was alone, and uncomfortable wondering what they were thinking or saying about me. We sometimes think people are thinking about us and talking about us all the time, but the truth is that most people are thinking about themselves and their situations. I was just plain ol' uncomfortable, hurting, and avoided. At least that's how I felt.

This experience taught me to be more mindful of what others are going through. I'm not perfect at all. I miss the mark and get caught up in the busyness of life, but I really try to stay connected knowing that one call or text could be the lifeline that another person needs.

Now, for anyone who is reading this, especially introverts, when you go through difficulty, please do not isolate yourself for extended periods of time. Find someone that you can talk to whether it's a friend, family member, counselor, or hotline. Do not leave yourself vulnerable for the enemy to whisper in your ear that your life isn't important and that you should end it.

Suicidal thoughts can have many different root causes. While I encourage prayer and reaching out to a friend for help, sometimes therapy and/or medication may be needed. Please don't be ashamed or embarrassed. Ultimately, it's about saving your life by any means necessary.

I believe very strongly that if churches do an altar call prayer for those who are having suicidal thoughts, there must be aftercare available to follow up. We have an obligation to follow up with anyone who self-identifies that they are thinking about self-harm.

If you find yourself in a situation where you are contemplating suicide, even if it's just for a moment, call someone immediately!

National Suicide Prevention Lifeline
Phone line available 24 hours:
800-273-8255
https://suicidepreventionlifeline.org/
The live chat hotline is also available 24 hours: https://suicidepreventionlifeline.org/chat

Chapter 6

Time to Heal

I AM AN INTROVERT.

I would love to tell you that after The Day, I was healed, filled with joy, and moved forward to pursue my purpose, but healing is a journey. During my healing journey, I had good days and bad days, but I survived so I won't complain. My last journal entry gives a little insight into my mindset at what felt like rock bottom to me:

Well, Lord, I guess the next stage has kicked into my human emotional state... numb. I am alone. I feel hopeless. God, I need you to help me. Please turn this around for me. I need you. I need your presence. I don't feel anything. Help me.

    I laid around a little more, especially since it was winter break. I didn't have to go to work, and my son was with my parents until the new year. So, I ate, slept, and watched TV. Then, God said, "Alright, it's time to get up." So, I did. I got up, did things around the house, started reading my Bible, and listened to uplifting music. My FAVORITE song was "Made a Way" by Travis Greene. That song was on heavy rotation and set the atmosphere for my healing.

    New Year's Eve church service was at a local hotel and I had no intention of attending... NONE! At the last minute, I decided to go, but I was not in a mood to socialize, so I sat way in the back hoping to blend in. Eventually, I felt so convicted about sitting back there, I ended up moving closer to the front and tried to shake it off. The message was just what I needed to hear to propel me forward into the new year.

Sometimes, you just have to decide to take up your bed and walk! (John 5:8) While you're distressed, sad, hurting, grieving, or ill, you still have to keep moving forward with life trusting that God is walking with you, guiding you, and making a way for you to overcome. I know that sounds cliché, but have you ever been ill and in bed for a day or two and felt better when you started moving around? There is something to be said for getting up and moving as a pivotal step in the healing process.

Pain, sickness, hurt, grief, embarrassment, and all the other feelings we have in times of distress are temporary. They feel like they will last forever, but the Bible says, "weeping may stay for the night, but rejoicing comes in the morning" (Psalm 30:5b). I learned that I had to trust God in a way that seemed impossible, knowing that there would be peace on the other side and that He always has a plan for me. These are some of the scriptures that I repeated to myself to keep me going and served as a reminder for me whenever my thoughts wandered.

Trust in the Lord with all your heart and lean not on your own understanding; in all your ways submit to him, and he will make your paths straight. (Proverbs 3:5-6)

Do not be anxious about anything, but in every situation, by prayer and petition, with thanksgiving, present your requests to God. And the peace of God, which transcends all understanding, will guard your hearts and minds in Christ Jesus. (Philippians 4:6-8)

"For I know the plans that I have for you," declares the Lord, "plans to prosper you and not to harm you, plans to give you hope and a future." (Jeremiah 29:11)

My next step was to figure out how to move forward. What was the purpose of this pain? What was my destiny? So, I picked up a book that I had on my shelf called "Roadmap to Destiny: A 21-Day Devotional for Those on the Pathway to Purpose" by Joy V. Morgan. That book helped change the trajectory of my life.Some of the nuggets that propelled me were:

- Don't focus on the big project. Just take one small step.
- Identify the one thing that only God can do.
- God knows about the detours and He is right there waiting for us to continue the journey.

There were so many more words of wisdom in the book, and I encourage you to read it for yourself. It was enough to give me the strength and courage to PUSH!

I had stopped my doctorate program after 9 years because I had been going through so much, had a balance of about $2,000, and did not have the money to pay it. So, I took my experience in higher education and a mustard seed of faith and wrote an email to the school asking them to waive the balance. I was honest with them about my situation and promised to graduate from the program. Within a few days, they responded with a "Yes!!!" They waived my entire balance, and the only caveat was that I had to take an additional course, which I started shortly thereafter.

Up until that point, I had been through two dissertation chairs, I had rewritten the first three chapters of my dissertation several times and was about to embark on this journey again. I found an amazing dissertation chair and we started working together.

By November, I submitted my dissertation proposal to the review board for approval. They returned it two weeks later; unapproved with revisions needed. On Sunday, March 5, 2017, at 5:25 p.m., I received my proposal back again for a third time; unapproved with revisions needed by midnight. Technically, the revisions amounted to about 3-5 pages and my chair thought that was great. However, I felt rejected (again) because I had rewritten and revised these three chapters more times than I care to remember. I tried to remember the key to dissertation success... perseverance and humility.

I had decided enough was enough. I was done. I was tired. In retrospect, it always amazes me how close we are to fulfilling goals when we decide to quit.

So, in my rebellion, I hopped on social media and decided to scroll my life away. As God would have it, I "stumbled" upon Denzel Washington's NAACP Image Award video that a friend posted. This video was so encouraging! In it, Denzel says something like "Ease is the greatest threat to progress than hardship... If you fall down seven times, get up eight."

After watching, I decided to just write those few pages and I submitted the revisions within minutes of the deadline. The next day, I received full approval to proceed with my dissertation research! Over the next few months, I conducted my research, wrote the remaining chapters, and submitted my completed dissertation to the review board. I will admit that I had quite a bit of anxiety because of my previous experiences on these submissions, but I received full approval of my dissertation and successfully defended the day before Thanksgiving. As I reflected on the journey and everything I overcame to accomplish that goal, I cried tears of joy and gratefulness to God for keeping me.

Even amid trying to move forward toward my destiny, I was still in pain, trying to find myself, trying to feel good, and trying to heal. I was also upset with God.

I know many won't admit that when they experience trauma or hurt, they may be upset that God allowed it to happen. Well, I will admit it. While I was going to church, trying to push past the pain, I wanted to feel loved again and was upset with God that I was single again. I had 2 engagements prior but didn't get married because there were serious issues in those relationships. I had waited for "the one" that I thought God had for me, and look how that turned out. It took me a long time to figure out that in the rebellion that followed my anger, I was hurting myself and delaying my healing.

Even through all of that, I met the love of my life on an online dating site. We have had our share of ups and downs while learning one another, cleaning up past baggage, and blending our families. I am grateful for a man who loves all my perfect imperfections; who gets this introvert out and about; has made it safe for me to be vulnerable; creates a fun, silly, and loving relationship; and supports every aspect of my life and purpose in God. I am forever grateful that John and I found one another, and I cannot wait to see what God has in store for us.

My post-doctoral story and destiny are still being written, literally. I have not yet arrived, but I feel healed from that trauma. I started each chapter with "*I AM AN INTROVERT*" because writing this story allowed me to recollect, reflect, and celebrate my life through the lens of that self-discovery.

My life is precious. All lives are precious.

What I have learned is that there is purpose in pain and there are lessons in the journey. Here are my takeaways:

1. Being good or nice does not exempt you from trials.

2. Trouble does not last always.

3. Joy is always right around the corner.

4. Problems and obstacles build character.

5. Pain and overcoming are testimonies meant to help someone else who may

be dealing with the same thing and feeling alone.

6. We are never alone.

7. It's OK to love Jesus and see a therapist.

8. Masks hinder breakthrough and healing. Remove the masks.

9. Never be ashamed to ask for help.

10. Your life matters.

11. Help is a prayer, phone call, or text message away.

12. Healing takes time. Give yourself time and permission to heal.

13. To heal, you must stop thinking and start feeling.

14. Music is therapeutic.

15. Great friendships are priceless.

16. Even when we can't see it or feel it, God is working.

17. Once you're healed, share your story, and help someone else.

18. Perseverance is faith and work in action.

19. Don't isolate yourself when you are going through difficulty even if you're an introvert.

20. Prayer changes things. Maintain a healthy prayer life, have at least a few friends in your life who know how to pray, and pray regularly for the strong, silent folks in your life.

And last, but absolutely not least...

INTROVERTS ROCK!!!!

References

[1] "Introversion." *Psychology Today,* accessed 13 Feb. 2021, https://www.psychologytoday.com/us/basics/introversion

[2] Beverly D. Flaxington. "Understanding Introverts: Being Quiet Is Not a Defect." *Psychology Today,* 15 Jan. 2016, https://www.psychologytoday.com/us/blog/understand-other people/201601/understanding-introverts

[3] Numbers 14:1-45

[4] Joyce Meyer in *Battlefield of the Mind: Winning The Battle in Your Mind* (New York: Faith Words, 2017), 7.

[5] Lana Burgess. "8 Benefits of Crying: Why Do We Cry, and When to Seek Support." *Medical News*

Today, 7 Oct. 2017, https://www.medicalnewstoday.com/articles/319631

[6] INFJ Male. "6 Reasons Why Introverts Hide Their Feelings." INFJ Male Psychology, 25 Nov. 2021, https://infjmalepsychology.com/6-reasons-why-introverts-hide-their-feelings/

About the Author

Photographer: Tanisha Dunham, LightLens Photography

Born and raised in Philadelphia, PA and now a resident of Norristown, PA, Dr. Christal L. Chatman is no stranger to the hallowed halls of academia. She has earned a BS in Accounting (Chestnut Hill College), an MBA in Human Resources (Keller Graduate School of Management), and a Doctor of Business Administration (University of Phoenix Online). With over 25 years of leadership, strategic planning, and professional development experience, Dr. Christal coaches individuals and teams and provides tools needed to improve team performance, manage change, develop a collaborative organizational culture, increase employee engagement, and excel as a leader.

Through Christal's leadership, the locations she's worked at have become stronger in organizational growth, customer retention, and employee engagement. She has also served as the Chair of her organization's employee engagement committee. She volunteers her time helping others with career transition and college planning and acts as an adjunct professor. One of her signature strengths is providing opportunities for learning, that can be applied in the workplace immediately.

In ministry, Dr. Christal has held the positions of Community Outreach Team Leader, Church Administrator, and currently, she is the co-leader of the Women's Ministry at Power in the Cross Ministries located in Norristown, PA. She has stepped from behind the desk and is excited to introduce her first book to us, "Behind the Mask: An Introvert's Perspective on Trauma, Perseverance, and Healing. She still continues to serve her students and the members of the church she attends.

Dr. Christal L. Chatman has a core belief that God has a purpose and destiny for each of us. She says, "The journey may have some detours and obstacles as it's meant to build character, faith, and trust in God. If we just keep pushing. praying, persevering, and handling each task, we will ultimately, achieve our goals and accomplish what we set out to do. Then...on to the next."

www.ingramcontent.com/pod-product-compliance
Lightning Source LLC
Chambersburg PA
CBHW071904070526
44583CB00016B/1838